THE TRIBULATION &
THE CHURCH

by Chuck Smith

Published by **The Word For Today**
P.O. Box 8000 Costa Mesa CA 92628
ISBN 0–936728–01–9

Table of Contents

THE TRIBULATION &
THE CHURCH
by Chuck Smith

"...For then shall be great tribulation, such as was not since the beginning of the world to this time, no, nor ever shall be." Matthew 24:21

Jesus answering the question, "What shall be the sign of Thy coming, and of the end of the world?"

INTRODUCTION

Can you imagine 50–pound chunks of ice falling out of the sky? Can you conceive of the devastation from a hailstorm with hailstones weighing 50 pounds? Where would you hide? How could you be safe? The hailstones would rip through the roof of your house as if it was paper. They would flatten your automobile. The hail would destroy and level almost everything. What could stand up under that kind of bombardment?

Can you picture the Sierra Nevada mountain range suddenly dropping to 5,000 feet below sea level? The Pacific Ocean would come rushing in to fill the resulting canyon. How could anyone on the West Coast escape? What would happen to the millions of people?

Can you conceive of a time when people couldn't die? Perhaps their bodies would be mangled in a plane crash, yet their spirits would refuse to leave.

They'd have to remain in a maimed condition for six months, waiting for death.

Such events will soon take place upon the earth. God will pour out His wrath upon the earth and the people who dwell upon it who have rejected His plan of salvation. From the prophecies that are being fulfilled on the earth today we believe that this Great Tribulation will begin soon.

There's a debate in theological circles as to whether or not the Church will be here when God's wrath is unleashed upon the earth. Many are saying the Church must go through this time period of judgment known as the Great Tribulation. They speak disparagingly of the blessed hope that Christ will come for His Church *before* God's judgments are loosed upon the earth. Since they maintain that there's to be no escape for the Church, they make the prayer Christ encouraged us to pray in Luke 21:36 meaningless.

The purpose of this book is to examine the biblical reasons why I feel the Church will *not* be here during the Great Tribulation.

CHAPTER 1
THE TWO TRIBULATIONS

The fact that a time of great tribulation is coming upon the earth is firmly established in the Scriptures. In Daniel 12:1 we read, "And there shall be a time of trouble, such as never was since there was a nation even to the same time, **and at that time thy people shall be delivered,** every one that shall be found written in the book." This mention of "the book" is, no doubt, a reference to the Book of Life. What a wonderful promise of deliverance!

In Matthew 24:21–22 Jesus Himself said, "For then shall be great tribulation, such as was not since the beginning of the world to this time, no, nor ever shall be. And except those days should be shortened, there should no flesh be saved; but for the elect's sake those days shall be shortened." The "elect" here refers to Israel, as evidenced by the context (verse 16, 20). Both Daniel and Jesus spoke about the same "time of trouble" and day of "great tribulation" to come upon the earth.

The Book of Revelation gives us many details about the events that will transpire on earth during this time of Great Tribulation. Chapter 6 begins with the opening of the seven seals of judgment. The Tribulation continues through the seven trumpet judgments and the seven vials of God's wrath that will be poured out. If you want to fully understand what this Great Tribulation will be like, read Revelation Chapters 6 through 19 at this point.

It's important to make a clear distinction about tribulations as taught in the Bible. There are two different types of tribulation. (1) The Great Tribulation referred to by Jesus and Daniel and detailed by John in the Revelation. (2) The Tribulation that Jesus promised would come to the Church.

Speaking to His disciples in John 16:33 Jesus said, "These things I have spoken unto you, that in Me ye might have peace. In the world ye shall have tribulation; but be of good cheer; I have overcome the world." The Church will have tribulation in the world. It's important to notice that the "tribulation" faced by the Church originates from the world and comes from the world system controlled by Satan. Satan is behind all the attacks on the Church.

Paul tells us that we're wrestling not against flesh and blood, but against principalities and powers, against the rulers of the darkness of this world, against spiritual wickedness in high places. Spirit forces are warring against the children of God, the source

of our tribulation is definitely the world
system governed by Satan.

The Great Tribulation that will come
upon the earth originates from Heaven.
God's wrath is poured out in judgment
against the sinners during this
Tribulation. When the sixth seal is
opened in Revelation 6:12, those on
the earth try to hide and they call for
the rocks and the mountains to fall
upon them and hide them from the
wrath of the Lamb for the great day of
His wrath has come, and they
question, "Who shall be able to stand?"
Revelation 11:18 declares, "Thy wrath
is come."

In Revelation 14:10 the Great
Tribulation is referred to as the
indignation and wrath of God. When
the seals are opened in Heaven
corresponding judgments come upon
the earth. The angels are given
trumpets in Heaven, and as they blow
the trumpets corresponding judgments
come upon the earth. The vials from
the living creatures are opened by the
seven angels, and again corresponding

judgments come upon the earth. All these judgments come from God and have their origin in Heaven. In Psalm 69:20-28 we have a prophecy concerning Jesus it speaks of His disciples forsaking Him in the hour of need and of vinegar being given Him for His thirst. It then calls for God to pour out His indignation and His wrathful anger upon those who had persecuted the One whom God had smitten. Indignation is a word used in the Old Testament especially to describe the time of the great tribulation. Isaiah 26:19,20; Isaiah 34:1-8; Jeremiah 10:10; Daniel 8:19; Daniel 11:36; Nahum 1:5,6; Zephaniah 3:8. Note that in Isaiah 66:14 that the hand of the Lord will be known toward His children but His indignation toward His enemies.

Paul tells us in Romans 2:6 that God will render to every man according to his deeds. To them who by patient continuance in well doing seek for glory and honor and immortality, eternal life: but to them that are contentious, and do not obey the truth but obey unrighteousness, indignation and wrath, tribulation and anguish upon every soul of man that doeth evil. Hebrews 10:27 speaks of the fiery indignation that will devour His adversaries.

The tribulation experienced by the child of God comes from the Satan–governed world. The Tribulation that is coming on the sinful world will come from God.

Why is this Great Tribulation coming? The Scripture says that its purpose is threefold: (1) to try men who dwell upon the earth (Revelation 3:10); (2) that God might vent His wrath upon the wicked (Revelation 15:7), and (3) to destroy those who destroyed the earth (Revelation 11:18). Those who fall in one or all of these categories will be on the earth to experience the Tribulation period.

In the Old Testament the Lord spoke to Abraham and told him of the impending judgment on the cities of Sodom and Gomorrah. In response Abraham challenged the fairness of

God. He asked, "Shall not the Lord of the earth be just? Would You destroy the righteous with the wicked?" What if there are 50 righteous? The Lord responded that if He found 50 righteous He would spare the city for the sake of the 50 righteous.

Notice the whole premise of Abraham's intercession with God was that it wouldn't be fair for God to judge the righteous with the wicked. If the judgment proceeds from God, then it surely wouldn't be fair for God to judge the righteous along with the wicked. No where in the scripture when we find judgment proceeding directly from God do we find the righteous being judged with the wicked.

When the angels arrived in Sodom, they couldn't even find the ten righteous for whom Abraham had interceded. So, they delivered the one righteous man, Lot, out of the city. Not until he was delivered did the judgment of God come. They declared in Genesis 19:22 that they could not do anything until he was safely out of the way.

In Luke 17 when Jesus makes reference to Lot's escape, Jesus clearly points out that in the same hour Lot was brought out of the city, the judgment of God fell. In II Peter 2 the apostle points out that the cities of Sodom and Gomorrah were destroyed, "making them an example." However, God delivered that righteous man, Lot, who was vexed by the way people were living around him. Then Peter goes on to say, "For God knows how to deliver the righteous...and to reserve the ungodly for the day of judgment" (II Peter 2:9).

We're told in I Thessalonians 5 that God has *not* appointed us unto wrath. Also, in Romans 5:9 we're told that "being now justified by His blood, we shall be saved from wrath through Him."

Any argument that might be developed to prove that the Church will go through the Great Tribulation and experience the wrath of God that is coming upon the earth must somehow explain the following point. When did God change His ways as to now punish the righteous with the wicked? It would be a change in God's nature to force His children to face the outpouring of His wrath. Yet, God said that He changes not (Malachi 3:6).

In deductive logic the most common form of reasoning is known as a syllogism. A syllogism consists of a major premise, a minor premise, and a conclusion. When one premise is negative and the other positive, only a negative conclusion can follow. For example, a major premise might be positive: all birds have wings. The minor premise is negative: dogs do not have wings. The conclusion must be negative: dogs are not birds.

Our major premise is negative: the Church is not appointed to wrath (Greek: orge). "We shall be saved from **wrath**" (Rom.5:9); "God has not appointed us to **wrath**" (I Thess. 5:9). The minor positive premise is: the Great Tribulation is a time of God's

wrath (orge). "Hide us from the face of Him that sitteth on the throne, and from the **wrath** of the Lamb, for the great day of His **wrath** is come" (Rev. 6:16–17). The conclusion must be negative and plain: the Church will not experience the Great Tribulation. To argue any differently is to defy logic, and one may as well seek to prove that a dog is a bird. No further argument to prove that the Church will not go through the Great Tribulation is necessary, yet the burden of evidence is overwhelming. So, let us go on.

CHAPTER 2
THE 70 WEEKS

Around 538 BC. the prophet Daniel was waiting upon God for possible special orders that God might have for him. Daniel realized that the 70 years of Babylonian captivity were about over. Suddenly, the angel Gabriel appeared to Daniel. In Daniel 9:24 Gabriel declared that 70 "weeks" (literally, "sevens," representing 7–year periods) were determined upon "thy people" (Israel) and upon "thy holy city" (Jerusalem) "to finish the transgression, to make an end to sins, to make reconciliation for iniquity, to bring in everlasting righteousness, to seal up the visions and prophecy [i.e., to complete or fulfill the visions and prophecies], and to anoint the most Holy." The angel went on to say that from the time that the commandment would go forth to restore and rebuild Jerusalem to the coming of the Messiah the Prince would be 7 sevens and 62 sevens, or a total of 69 sevens. Since each seven represents a 7–year period, 69 sevens would be 483 years.

In his book, The Coming Prince,1 Sir Robert Anderson explains that this period would have to be predicated on the Babylonian calendar of 360 days per year. Thus, 483 years would be 173,880 days. On March 14, 445 BC., King Artaxerxes of Persia gave the commandment to Nehemiah to restore and rebuild Jerusalem. 173,880 days later brings us to April 6, 32 AD. This was the date when Christ made His triumphant entry into the city of Jerusalem (according to Anderson's calculation).2

The first part of the prophecy given to Daniel was fulfilled literally to the day. But the angel went on to say that the

Messiah would be "cut off, but not for Himself [literally, 'without receiving anything for Himself']: and the people of the prince that shall come shall destroy the city and the sanctuary." The destruction of the city referred to the sacking of Jerusalem under Titus in 70 AD. Titus was the general of the Roman legions, but he wasn't the prince of the people. Nero was the prince who ordered the destruction, though he died before the ravaging of Jerusalem was completed.

The city of Jerusalem and the sanctuary of the people were destroyed as the angel declared,, and the Jews were dispersed. Thus far, we see the marvelously accurate fulfillment of this prophecy in history. However, Gabriel said that 70 sevens were determined upon Israel. Messiah was cut off after 69 sevens. Where then is the seventieth seven?

In Daniel 9:27 the angel speaks again about the prince, using the pronoun "he." "He shall confirm the covenant with many for one week." The 69 "weeks" were to last from the commandment to restore and rebuild Jerusalem to the coming of Jesus Christ. As predicted, the Messiah was "cut off" without receiving the Kingdom, and the Jews were dispersed. The seventieth and final "week" of Daniel is still in the future.

Jesus referred to this prophetic "week" in Matthew 24. The disciples asked Him about the signs of His coming and the end of the age. In verse 15 Jesus said, "When ye therefore shall see the abomination of desolation, spoken of by Daniel the prophet, standing in the holy place, (whoso readeth, let him understand:) then let them which be in Judea flee into the mountains: let him which is on the housetop not come down to take anything out of his house." Then Jesus predicted a time of "great tribulation" such as the world has never seen before or will ever see again. This abomination that triggers the desolation takes place in the middle of the 70th 7.

Daniel speaks of this "abomination of desolation" in chapter 9. The prince of the people will "confirm the covenant with many for one week [seven years]: and in the midst of the week he shall cause the sacrifice and the oblation to cease, and for the overspreading of abomination he shall make it desolate, even until the consummation, and that determined shall be poured upon the desolate." Since Jesus referred to this final seven–year period as yet future in His day, and inasmuch as the Antichrist hasn't yet made the covenant with Israel, we must conclude that it's still in the future. The fact that the Antichrist makes the covenant for seven years indicates that it's signed at the beginning of the final seven–year period.

Halfway through the seven years the Antichrist will break the covenant with Israel, as he causes the daily sacrifices and oblations in the Temple to cease. According to Daniel 12:11, from that precise day until the end will be 1,290 days. Then Jesus will return again with His Church in the clouds with great glory. Paul said, "And when Christ who is our life shall appear, then shall you also appear with Him in glory."

The Church Age fits between the sixty–ninth and seventieth week of Daniel's prophecy. According to Paul in Ephesians 3:5 this mystery was hidden from the Old Testament writers. At the present time God has poured out His Spirit of grace upon the Gentiles, from whom He is drawing a bride for His Son. When the fullness of the Gentiles is come in, God will then catch up His Church, the waiting Bride. This is commonly called the Rapture of the Church.

CHAPTER 3
THE RAPTURE OF THE CHURCH

The Rapture will take place when Jesus Christ snatches His Church out of this world. It shall happen suddenly and without any notice. It's important to realize that the Rapture of the Church and the Second Coming of Jesus Christ are completely different. At the Rapture Jesus is Coming for His saints. At the Second Coming the Church will return with Jesus Christ. Jude 14 tells us, "Behold, the Lord cometh with ten thousands of His saints."

In I Corinthians 15:51–52 Paul said, "Behold, I show you a mystery; we will not all sleep, but we will be changed (there will be a metamorphosis, a change of body) in a moment, in the twinkling of an eye." You won't even realize what's happened until it's all over. Suddenly, you're in the presence of the Lord in your glorified body with all the Church!

We, the Church, will be changed. Paul wrote to the Philippians, "For our citizenship is in heaven, from whence we look for the Saviour, our Lord Jesus Christ: Who will change our vile body, that it may be fashioned like unto His glorious image" (Phil. 3:20–21). Describing the metamorphosis Paul wrote to Corinth, "For this corruption must put on incorruption, and this mortal must put on immortality" (I Cor. 15:53).

Speaking to the Thessalonians Paul said, "For the Lord Himself shall descend from heaven with a shout, with the voice of the archangel, and with the trump if God: and the dead in Christ shall rise first: then we which are alive and remain shall be caught up together with them in the clouds, to meet the Lord in the air: and so shall we ever be with the Lord. Wherefore comfort one another with these words" (I Thess. 4:16–18).

Some people would ridicule the idea or concept of the Rapture of the Church. They declare that the word "rapture" isn't even found in the Bible. It all depends on which version of the Bible you're reading.

The phrase "caught up" in I Thessalonians 4:17 is the Greek word harpazo, which actually means "to be snatched away with violent force." The Latin equivalent of harpazo is the verb rapio, "to take away by force." In the Latin Vulgate, one of the oldest Bibles in existence, the appropriate tense of rapio appears in verse 17. Raptus is the past participle of rapio, and our English words "rapt" and "rapture" stem from this past participle. Although "rapture" isn't in the king James Bible, the basic word does appear in the Latin Vulgate.

As for the time of the rapture, Jesus said, "No man knows the day or hour." For us to presume to declare some date or hour for the Rapture would be an unscriptural presumption. If we say we know the hour, we're boasting of knowledge superior to Christ's when He was upon the earth.

Although we don't know the exact time of the Rapture, in I Thessalonians 5 Paul said, "But of the times and seasons, brethren, you have no need that I write unto you. For you yourselves know perfectly that the day of the Lord is coming as a thief in the night. For when they will say, Peace and safety; then comes sudden destruction... But ye, brethren, are not in darkness, that that day should overtake you as a thief." The Bible is saying that the Rapture of the Church shouldn't come to you as a surprise.

God has given to us the signs that would precede the coming of Jesus Christ. One of the greatest signs to the world today is the reestablishment of the nation Israel. For years Bible scholars had looked forward to the regathering of the nation Israel based on many Scriptures (including Matthew 24:32) and the application of expositional constancy (fig tree or figs in parables symbolize the nation Israel). Skeptics ridiculed this prophecy. Never in history had a nation been born out of the past but a miracle has taken place and a nation has been reborn. God has reestablished Israel among the family of nations on the earth. God has fulfilled His promise.

Psalm 102:16 declares, "When the Lord shall build up Zion, He shall appear in His glory." Because the Lord is building up Zion, the orthodox Jews today are looking for their Messiah. We are too! We're looking forward to this fulfillment of God's promise – the coming again of our great God and Saviour Jesus Christ.

After the Church is raptured, God will once again deal with Israel, His elect. God will fulfill the many promises and prophecies of the Old

Testament that relate to Israel, including the seventieth week of Daniel. thus, one more seven–year period is to be fulfilled in Israel's history. Jeremiah calls it "the time of Jacob's trouble." Israel will experience God's preserving power during the Great Tribulation as 144,000 Jews will be sealed by God. Though on earth, they'll be shielded from part of the judgments (Revelation 7:3, 9:4).

The book of Revelation is divided into three general sections. In Revelation 1:19 the angel instructed John to write the things that he had seen, the things that are, and the things that shall be after these things. The Greek for "after these things" is meta tauta. In chapter 1 John wrote the vision which he saw: Christ in His resurrected glory standing in the midst of the seven golden candle sticks and holding the seven stars in His right hand. In chapters 2 and 3 John wrote of the things which are: the messages of Jesus Christ to the seven churches of

Asia (which also represent the seven periods of Church history).

Chapter 4 begins the third section of the Revelation. The chapter begins with the same Greek phrase, meta tauta, "after these things." The question naturally arises, "After what things?" The obvious answer is, "After the things of chapters 2 and 3." The things of the Church. So, you could begin Revelation 4:1, "After the things of the Church, I saw a door open in Heaven, and the first voice I heard was as a trumpet saying to me, Come up hither, and I will show you things which must be [then another repetition of meta tauta after these things]." This I believe is the account of the rapture of the church; the voice as of a trumpet calling the saints to come up. Paul speaks of the trumpet of God accompanying the rapture of the church. I Thessalonians 4:16; I Corinthians 15:52

The open door in Heaven takes us back to the message of Jesus to the Philadelphia church, His faithful and true remnant in the last days. He said, "I have set before thee an open door which no man can shut." Now this door is opened in Heaven, and the voice is calling as a trumpet."

The message to the church of Thyatira warned that a portion of that church would go through the Great Tribulation. Jesus said that He had this against them, because they allowed the woman, Jezebel, to teach and seduce His servants to commit fornication and to eat things that had been sacrificed to idols. He gave her space to repent of her fornication, and she repented not. Therefore, He was going to cast her into a bed and them that commit adultery with her into great tribulation, unless they repented of their deeds.

Here the warning to the church is definitely to repent or face the Great Tribulation. The obvious inference is that they could escape the Great Tribulation if they would repent.

In Revelation 3:10 the Lord addressing the church in Philadelphia said, "Because thou hast kept the word of My patience, I also will keep thee from the hour of temptation, which will come upon all the world, to try them that dwell upon the earth." This is a definite promise that His church would escape the Tribulation. I must concur that at least part of the Church will face the Great Tribulation. The unrepentant of the Church of Thyatira, who will not turn from their spiritual fornication, will go through the Tribulation and miss the Rapture.

As we move along in the Book of Revelation, chapter 4 gives us a description of the throne of God. We see the 24 elders sitting on their lesser thrones and living creatures, which are the cherubim. We also see a picture of the heavenly praise and worship of God.

In chapter 5 we see a scroll with writing on both sides, sealed with seven seals. An angel proclaims with a strong voice, "Who is worthy to take the scroll and loose the seals?" We see John sobbing convulsively, because no man is found worthy to take the scroll and loose the seals. We hear one of the elders comforting John telling him that the Lion of the tribe of Judah has prevailed to open the scroll and loose the seals. Then Jesus, the Lion of the tribe of Judah, steps forth looking like a Lamb that had been slaughtered. He takes the scroll out of the right hand of the Father. Then we hear the song of the redeemed in Heaven. They are singing a new song. "Thou art worthy to take the scroll and to open the seals thereof: for Thou wast slain, and hast redeemed us to God by Thy blood out of every kindred, and tongue, and people, and nation; and hast made us unto our God kings and priests; and we shall reign on the earth."

Some scholars argue that the lyrics of the song should read, "For Thou wast slain and hast redeemed them to God." In a few, I believe just 5 of the old manuscripts, from the Alexandrian School of Texts, the text reads "them" instead of "us." However, the vast majority, over 1,000 of old manuscripts the majority text or Textus Receptus reads as translated in the King James Version. The text is rightfully translated, "redeemed us to God."

Who can sing of redemption through the blood of Jesus Christ from all of the nations and families of people upon the earth? Obviously, only one group can sing that song, the Church. In Luke's gospel Chapter 21 where Jesus is sharing with His disciples the signs of His second coming, He speaks of the events of the great tribulation that shall precede His return. he then said, "Pray always that you may be accounted worthy to escape all these things that shall come to pass, (i.e. the things that will transpire in the great tribulation) and to stand before the Son of Man." That is exactly what we see here in Revelation 5, the church standing before the Son of Man, the Lamb of God, in heaven.

It is significant that the Church is singing before the throne of God the song of praise to Jesus Christ before He ever opens a single seal of the scroll. The Church is singing in Heaven before the Great Tribulation ever starts. The Church as a group isn't seen on the earth again in the Book of Revelation, until the Church comes back to earth riding on white horses with Jesus Christ in Revelation 19.

The group in Heaven in chapter 7 which came up out of the Great Tribulation isn't the Church. John didn't recognize them when the elder asked him, "Who are these?" Their position isn't the same as the Church's. This group stands in the holy Temple and serves God day and night continually, whereas the Church sings of the glorious prospect of reigning with Christ.

Chapter 13 of the Book of Revelation refers to the coming of the man of sin who makes "war with the saints." These "saints" couldn't be the Church saints, because the man of sin overcomes them.

Daniel also testified to this fact. Daniel 7:21 describes the "little horn," the Antichrist. "I beheld, and the same horn made war with the saints, and prevailed against them." However, Jesus said that the gates of hell wouldn't prevail against His Church, Matthew 16:18. It's impossible that the saints of Revelation 13 and Daniel 7 could be in the Church, because the Antichrist cannot triumph over the Church.

This is another syllogism with negative and positive premises and it can only produce a negative conclusion. Major premise: the gates of hell cannot prevail against the Church. Minor premise: the saints are overcome by the Antichrist. Conclusion: the saints are not the Church. The saints must then be Israel, which are also the "elect" of Matthew 24:31.

Chapter 5
The Restraining Force

In II Thessalonians Paul the apostle wrote to correct an error that had crept into the Church. Some false teachers were saying that the day of the Lord had already come. Paul told the Thessalonians that "that day," the Second Coming of Jesus Christ to reign over the earth, wouldn't take place until there was first a falling away, or departure, and the man of sin, the son of perdition, was revealed. Paul reminded the believers that he had told them these things when he was with them.

In chapter 2 Paul declared, "Now you know what is withholding him that he might be revealed in his time. But the mystery of iniquity is already at work; only he who is restraining will continue to restrain, until he is taken out of the way. And then shall that wicked one be revealed, whom the Lord will consume with the Spirit of His mouth, and shall destroy with the brightness of His coming."

Who is the "restraining" force holding back the revelation of the Antichrist? I believe that the restraining force is the power of the Holy Spirit working in and through the Church. As long as the Spirit filled Church is upon the earth, the unveiling of the Antichrist will be held back. As soon as the Church is taken out of the way, nothing will stand in the way of the Antichrist. He'll then take over the governments of the world.

The Holy Spirit will not be removed from the world, for He is omnipresent. However, during this time He will be poured out upon Israel.

Ezekiel 39:29 says that God will put His Spirit upon the nation Israel at the time the Russian army is destroyed. This event will possibly mark the beginning of the final seven–year period determined upon Israel.

I see the whole picture coming together very beautifully. After the Church is removed, the Antichrist will be revealed. In Revelation 6 the first event that takes place when the seven–sealed scroll is opened is the white horse coming forth with his rider. This apparently is the Antichrist coming upon the earth. Since the Church has been removed and is now rejoicing with the Lord in Heaven, nothing restrains this wicked one from moving out and taking over the world.

Those who teach that the Church must go through the Great Tribulation and face the wrath of God which is coming upon the earth try to identify the last trump of I Corinthians 15 with the seventh trumpet in the Book of Revelation. I see great difficulties in paralleling these two trumpets.

First of all, the trumpet that sounds at the time of the Rapture of the Church in I Thessalonians 4:16 is called the "trump of God." In Revelation the seventh trumpet is the trumpet of the seventh angel.

The trump of I Corinthians 15 is used to proclaim an event that happens in a moment, in a twinkling of an eye, at the last trump." On the other hand, the seventh trump of the Book of Revelation will cover a period of days. Revelation 10:7 says, "But in the days [plural]

of the voice of the seventh angel, when he shall begin to sound, the mystery of God should be finished, as He hath declared to His servants the prophets."

The last trump of I Corinthians 15 and I Thessalonians 4 will be a trumpet of glory. We shall be changed and made into His image and caught up to meet the Lord in the air. However, the seventh trumpet of the Book of Revelation is continually referred to as a woe. In Revelation 8:13 the angel said, "Woe, woe, woe, to the inhabitants of the earth by reason of the other three voices of the trumpet of the three angels, which are yet to sound!" The angel says this at the end of the fourth trumpet. So, the three "woes" refer to the fifth, sixth, and seventh trumpets. At the end of the fifth trumpet (Revelation 9:12), the angel declares, "One woe is past; and, behold, there come two woes more hereafter." This refers to the sixth and seventh trumpets. In Revelation 11:14 the angel declares that the second woe is past and, behold, the third woe comes quickly. Then we go right into verse 15, the seventh trumpet, which is actually the third woe.

The Rapture of the Church and being changed into His glorious likeness is far from a woe. It would only be a woe if I didn't go! Thus, I see great difficulty in identifying the seventh trumpet of Revelation 15 and the last trumpet of I Corinthians 15 as one an the same, because the results and the time factors are so different. In his New Testament Greek commentary on I Corinthians 15:52, Dean Henry Alford declares that no reason exists to define the last trump to be the seventh trumpet of Revelation.(1) He also says that there's no reason to assume that

there are no trumpets after the last
trump of I Corinthians 15.

CHAPTER 7

THE FIRST RESURRECTION

Another major argument used by those who teach that the Church will go through the Great Tribulation centers around Revelation 20:4–5. John said, "I saw thrones, and they sat upon them, and judgment was given upon them; and I saw the souls of them that were beheaded for the witness of Jesus, and for the Word of God, and which had not worshipped the beast, neither his image, neither had received his mark upon their foreheads, or in their hands; and they lived and reigned with Christ a thousand years. But the rest of the dead lived not again until the thousand years were finished. This is the first resurrection."

The argument presented is that "first resurrection" means there was no resurrection prior to it. First means first, and nothing could be before it. However, if you try to make the first resurrection all take place in Revelation 20 after Satan is bound and cast into the *abusso* for a thousand years, you must somehow explain why Jesus was called the "firstfruits of those who rise from the dead." Did not Jesus already rise?

Also, there's a great multitude in Heaven in Revelation 7 crying, "Salvation to our God which sits upon the throne, and unto the Lamb." When the elder asked John, "Who are these arrayed in white robes? And where did they come from?" John answered that he didn't know. The elder responded, "These are they which have come out of the great tribulation, and have washed their robes, and made them white in the blood of the Lamb. Therefore are they before the throne of

God, and serve Him day and night in His temple." Here in chapter 7 is a multitude in Heaven who have come out of the Great Tribulation, thus resurrected before Revelation 20.

In Revelation 15 we see another company in Heaven. John describes the sea of glass mingled with fire, and he sees those who had gained victory over the beast, over his image, over his mark, and over the number of his name. They're standing on the sea of glass having the harps of God. They're singing the song of Moses, the servant of God. So, these would be the redeemed of Israel who had gained victory over the beast. John sees them in Heaven before the seven final vials of God's wrath are poured out.

Here are two resurrected companies in Heaven who have had a part in the first resurrection – prior to Revelation 20 when John sees those who had been beheaded for their witness of Jesus and refers to the "first resurrection."

In Revelation 20:4 John sees two distinct different companies. First of all, he sees thrones and those who sat upon them. Judgment was given to them. No doubt, this is the Church. The Lord made a promise to those who would overcome in the church of Laodicea. He promised to grant to them that they should sit with Him in His throne, even as He also overcame and has sat down with His Father in His throne. John sees a second company in Revelation 20:4. They're the souls of those who were beheaded for the witness of Jesus, who hadn't worshipped the beast, neither his image, neither had received his mark on their foreheads. These are definite, separate companies. One is sitting upon its thrones; the other came up out of the Great Tribulation, having been delivered from the power of the Antichrist and not yielding to his rule.

The first resurrection takes place over a period of time. Those who advocate that the Church will go through this time of God's wrath say that the first resurrection is the resurrection of the last day. They insist on a literal 24-hour day. The first resurrection actually covers a period of time and encompasses many different events. There are those who rose when Jesus rose from the dead (Matthew 27:52); those coming back with Christ when He comes to catch us away to meet Him in the air (I Thess. 4:14), and those who are martyred for their testimony of Jesus Christ and who will rise during the period of the Great Tribulation. They all have a part in the first resurrection. The first resurrection exists in contradistinction to the second resurrection, the resurrection of the unjust to stand before the Great White Throne judgment of God.

CHAPTER 8
WATCH & BE READY

It's obvious that Jesus intended His disciples and the Church in each age to be anticipating His return at any time for them. His word to the disciples was to watch and be ready; for they wouldn't know the day or the hour when He was coming, and He was coming at a time when they wouldn't expect. Therefore, they should always be watching and ready.

If you argue that the Church must go through the Great Tribulation, then you're taking away from the imminency of the return of Jesus Christ. The Church will not be watching, nor do we have any need to be watching for His return, if we must first go through the Great Tribulation. In that case, we'd be watching for the Great Tribulation or the unveiling of the Antichrist. The Church would then have many things to watch for, and we could actually follow the final events rather carefully.

The first major event would be the unveiling of the Antichrist. He would establish his reign and institute his new monetary system. Christians would then have to devise some way to survive without buying or selling. Next, we would watch for the great judgments predicted to come upon the earth. We would be especially watching for the Antichrist to stand in the Holy of Holies of the rebuilt Temple, proclaim himself to be God, and stop the daily sacrifices and prayers. According to Daniel, we know from that point that the Lord would be returning in 1,290 days (Daniel 12:11).

The Bible says that no man knows the day or the hour. This cannot refer to the day Christ returns to reign on earth, because that exact day has been give to us in Daniel's prophecy. No man knows the day or the hour when the Lord will take His Church out of the earth. Therefore, we must be watching – not for the Tribulation or the unveiling of the Antichrist – but for Jesus Christ to come for us at any time!

In Matthew 24:42 Jesus begins His exhortations to watch and be ready by giving a series of parables.

The first is an allegory concerning the goodman of the house. If the man had only known in what hour the thief was going to come, he would have watched and wouldn't have allowed his house to be broken into. "Therefore," Jesus said, "be ready, for in such an hour as you think not the Son of man comes."

Then Jesus gave the parable of the faithful and wise servant. His lord had made him the ruler over the household, and when the lord comes he will find him so doing, that is, watching in readiness.

Jesus warned about the evil servant who would say in his heart, "My lord delays his coming." I believe that any time you teach that the Rapture cannot take place until after the Tribulation or after the revelation of the Antichrist, you're saying in effect that the Lord is delaying His coming, at least until the unveiling of the Antichrist or the great tribulation is over.

Jesus warns us that such a belief led to slothfulness by the servant. The lord came in an hour when the servant wasn't expecting him. The servant was given his portion with the unbelievers. In contrast, believing that the Lord could come at any moment tends toward diligence and purity. In I John 3:2 we are told that now we are the sons of God and it does not yet appear what we shall be, however, when He appears we will be like Him, for we will see Him as He is. We are then told that he who has this hope purifies himself even as He is pure. The whole concept again is that the Lord wants us to be watching and ready for His coming –

not watching for the Tribulation or its beginning, or for the Antichrist or his revelation.

Be watching for Jesus Christ to come for us at any moment. To put any event before the coming of Christ for His Church is, in essence, saying that the Lord will delay His coming until after that event has happened. Teaching this is very dangerous, and Jesus Himself warned.

Through Matthew 25 Jesus emphasizes the necessity of being ready. In the parable of the ten virgins, the five foolish virgins weren't ready for the Lord when He came. When the cry went forth, "Behold, the Bridegroom cometh," those who were ready went in. In verse 13 Jesus said, "Watch therefore, for ye know neither the day nor the hour wherein the Son of man cometh."

We firmly believe that the coming of Christ is imminent, that not one single prophecy must be fulfilled before He catches up His Church, and that He has intended the Church of every generation to be watching and waiting for His return. In Mark 13:35-37 Jesus said, "Watch ye therefore: for you know not when the Master of the house cometh, at evening, or at midnight, or at the cockcrowing, or in the morning: lest, coming suddenly, He finds you sleeping. And what I say unto you I say unto all, Watch."

The Lord has given us some special promises relating to the Great Tribulation and the Church. The first promise is in Revelation 3:10 to His faithful church of Philadelphia. "Because you have kept the word of My patience, I will also keep you from the hour of temptation which will come to try men who dwell upon the earth." Interpreting this verse to mean that Jesus would keep us in the Tribulation and take us through it by divine preservation is totally without solid scriptural foundation and lacks sound scholarship. Such an interpretation is reading into a Scripture something that isn't there in order to harmonize it with a presuppositional view. Nowhere does the Book of Revelation speak about any divine preservation for the Church. The only divine preservation is for 144,000 Israelites who are sealed and, thus, spared from a portion of the judgments to come. Also, the woman of Chapter 12 is given wings of an eagle to bear her into the wilderness to escape from the wrath of the dragon for 3 1/2 years.

In I Thessalonians 5:9 Paul wrote about the coming of Christ for His Church. "For God has not appointed us to wrath, but to obtain salvation by our Lord Jesus Christ." It's totally inconsistent with the nature of God to think that after Jesus bore completely the judgment for my sins, God would have me judged with the wicked world. God's wrath and judgment will be poured out upon a Christ rejecting world. As a child of God, why would God number me with the unrighteous? God has not appointed us unto wrath.

Another interesting promise is found in Isaiah 26:19–21. The Lord first speaks of the resurrection of the dead. Then He said, "Come, my people, enter into thy chambers, and shut thy doors about thee: hide thyself as it were for a little moment, until the indignation be overpast. For, behold, the Lord cometh out of his place to punish the inhabitants of the earth for their iniquity: the earth also shall disclose her blood, and shall no more cover her slain."

Isaiah is prophesying of the day when the Lord comes to punish the inhabitants of the earth, the Great Tribulation period. But God invites His people to enter into His chambers and shut the doors about them, so they might be hid as it were for a moment until the indignation, the Tribulation, is over.

This could refer to the Jews who will flee to the rock city of Petra and be preserved from the Great Tribulation. Isaiah also mentions this in chapter 16. "Let mine outcasts dwell with thee,

Moab; be thou a covert to them from the face of the spoiler: for the extortioner is at an end, the spoiler ceaseth, the oppressors are consumed out of the land. And in mercy shall the throne be established: and he shall sit upon it in truth in the tabernacle of David, judging, and seeking judgment, and hasting righteousness."

In this text the people of Moab are told to take the Jews and shelter them in Sela, which is Petra, during the time when the Antichrist will try to destroy the Jews. If this promise of preservation refers to the Jews instead of the Church, why would the Lord shield the Jews and not the Church from the Great Tribulation?

If the Lord plans to shield the Church from the Great Tribulation, then where are the promises? Where does the Bible show the Church as being sealed, protected, or marked, so that it wouldn't be harmed during the Great Tribulation? As John clearly details the events of the last days in the Book of Revelation, what passages tell of the

Church's preservation in the Tribulation?

In Luke 21 Jesus is talking about the Great Tribulation and His coming again. He tells us, "Take heed, lest at any time your hearts be overcharged with surfeiting, and drunkenness, and the cares of this world, so that day come upon you unawares. For as a snare shall it come on all them that dwell on the face of the whole earth." Then again, "Watch ye therefore, and pray always, that ye may be accounted worthy to escape all these things that shall come to pass."

Escape all *what* things that shall come to pass? Surely I don't want to escape the Lord's coming for His Church. Jesus was referring to the Great Tribulation that is coming, and I'd surely like to escape that! I'm praying and watching just as Jesus told me to. "May I be accounted worthy to escape all these things of the Great Tribulation and stand before the Son of man"

I expect to stand before the throne of God in the great multitude of Revelation 5 when Jesus takes the scroll out of the right hand of Him who is sitting upon the throne. I don't expect to be on earth when the seals are opened and God begins to pour out His wrath and indignation upon this godless, Christ rejecting world. This makes the coming of Christ a blessed hope for the believers. We're passionately looking for that blessed hope, the glorious appearing of our great God and Saviour Jesus Christ. The Old Testament gives us the accounts of two times when the earth was judged by God. The flood of Noah's day and the fire and brimstone that destroyed Sodom at the time of Lot. Jesus likened both of these times to the time of His return. "As the days of Noah were, so shall also the coming of the Son of Man be." Matthew 24:37. In Luke 17:28,29 "As it was in the days of Lot; they did eat, they drank, they bought, they sold, they planted, they built; but the same day that Lot went out of Sodom it rained fire and brimstone from heaven." In both cases the righteous were delivered before the judgment of God came. Noah was a type of the 144,000 sealed by God, so to speak, in the ark and protected in the judgment, Lot's type of the church delivered from the judgment. We also have the case of the three Hebrew children in Daniel who were protected in the fiery furnace. The question is, "Where was Daniel?" Do you think he bowed to Nebuchadnezzar's image? I think not, he is mysteriously away. Many believe that the image of Nebuchadnezzar was a type of the image of the beast in Revelation 13, the 3 Hebrew children the type of faithful Israel protected in the tribulation and Daniel a type of the church protected from the tribulation.

One word should be said concerning the argument that the Rapture isn't a traditionally historic Church doctrine. If we look at the traditional church history and if we consider the church in the New Testament as being a part of the historic church, I believe that the Scriptures clearly indicate that the early Church was looking for the imminent return of Jesus Christ. The Christians were expecting Him to come at any time for them. In I Thessalonians 4 the believers were sorrowing over their loved ones who had died before the Lord returned, thinking they were going to miss the kingdom age.

Paul said to the Phillipians, "For our citizenship is in Heaven; from whence also we look for our Lord and Saviour Jesus Christ, who when He comes will change these vile bodies that they might be fashioned like unto His own glorious image." It's true that the anticipation of the return of the Lord waned during much of the Church's history, especially during the Dark Ages.

Moreover, there are many things in historic Church doctrine with which I don't agree. Historic Church doctrine teaches baptismal regeneration of infants. I don't believe that the Bible teaches baptismal regeneration of infants. The historic Church teaches the intercession of Mary and the dead saints. I don't believe that the Bible teaches the intercession of the dead saints or Mary. The historic Church teaches the infallibility of the pope. I don't believe in the infallibility of the pope. There are many things in historic Church doctrine that I feel aren't scriptural and I don't agree with. I don't look at historic Church doctrine as correct in every form and concept, nor do I see the historic Church as a model for us to practice or follow. The only true model is found in the book of Acts. By the time John wrote the book of Revelation, so much false doctrine had crept in that over and over Jesus was calling on the church to repent. Revelation 2 and 3.

There are claims that the interest in the Rapture and its teachings grew out of the Plymouth Brethren. The story goes that in a meeting in England a woman began to exhort the Church through the gift of prophecy, and she said that the Lord was going to take His Church out and save it from the wrath to come. We're told that men like

Darby and Scofield then began to popularize this view.

In Daniel 12 the prophet was seeking an understanding from God as to the time of the end. the Lord told Daniel to "shut up the words, and seal the book, even to the time of the end; many shall run to and fro, and knowledge shall be increased." The increased knowledge in the context of Daniel 12 is the knowledge of the prophetic truth that had been sealed till the time of the end.

As we're approaching the day in which the Lord is to take his Church out of this world, it would only be fitting that He make us more aware of the promise to the Church of being caught up before the Great Tribulation. Why would the Lord reveal it to Luther, Calvin, or any Reformation Church leaders? They weren't living in the age when the Church was to be taken out.

The Book of Daniel was to be sealed until the time of the end, and we're now in that time. Daniel 12:4 definitely promises that the knowledge of prophecy will be increased. It's only right to assume that God would be giving us new insights into the understanding of His promises and of His Word in these days in which we live.

I don't know of any liberal Church theologian who believes in the Rapture of the Church. However, it's a hope held by the vast majority of evangelical Christians throughout the world – for we truly believe that Jesus Christ is coming soon, and we look for Him to take us out of this wicked world system at any time.

Even so, come quickly, Lord Jesus!

CHAPTER 10
PREPARATION

In the light of the fact that the Lord might come even today, what should I do as a Christian?

First, let me tell you what you shouldn't do. Don't quit your job, sell your house, or see how much money you can borrow figuring you won't have to pay it back. Jesus said, "Occupy until I come" (Luke 19:13). He intends for us to go right on in our work. With both Noah and Lot it was business as usual right up to the day God delivered them.

Jesus said, "Watch" (Matt.24:42). You should be watching. The Scripture says, "And unto them that look for Him shall He appear the second time" (Heb. 9:28). You should be ready. Jesus said, "Therefore be ye also ready, for in such an hour as you think not the Son of man cometh" (Matt. 24:44). Amos cried out, "Prepare to meet thy God" (Amos 4:12). You need to prepare. That preparation is in giving your heart and life to Jesus Christ, receiving His forgiveness and the blotting out of your sins and transgressions. And then wait. James said, "Be patient therefore, brethren, unto the coming of the Lord, behold the husbandman waiteth for the precious fruit of the earth, and hath long patience for it.....be ye also patient....for the coming of the lord draweth nigh" (James 5:7-8). II Peter 3:3-4 tells us that in the last days there would be scoffers who would say, "Where's the promise of His coming?" But "God is not slack concerning His promises, as some men count slackness; but He is faithful to us, not willing that any should perish" (v.9)

At times there may be a hesitancy in our hearts concerning the coming of

Jesus Christ because of what will happen to our unsaved family members when He returns.

Once we've been caught up, it is possible that many of our loved ones who have been hassled by our witness and upset with our testimony will realize that they've actually missed the opportunity of being raptured with the Church. As a result, they'll become deadly serious with God and will choose to be martyred during the Great Tribulation period by refusing to take the mark of the beast. They'll choose death in preference to the mark and thus, be saved. (Rev. 20:4). Because of the teaching of Paul in II Thessalonians some doubt that anyone who has rejected the truth now will be able to believe the truth then. It definitely is a question and when my eternal destiny is at stake I do not want any questions, only certainty.

In Revelation 7:9–14 John saw in heaven "a great multitude which no man could number, of all nations and kindreds...clothed with white robes," singing of salvation. Concerning this great multitude the elder said to John, "These are they which came up out of **the great tribulation**, and washed their robes and made them white in the blood of the Lamb." In Revelation 6:9–11 under the fifth seal, these souls martyred during the Tribulation period are waiting for their opportunity to enter the heavenly scene. They're told to wait a little longer until the total number be slain as they were slain.

Being a Tribulation saint is a hard way to come. As Jesus said, "For then will be great tribulation" such as the world never has seen before or ever will see again (Matt. 24:21). *Why wait?* Why put off your chances of knowing the glorious excitement of being with the Lord when He catches up the Church?

The question at this point is, "Are you ready?" Consider the Lord proclaiming today, "This is the end for the Church! You have finished your witness. Come home!" Would you be gathered with the Church to meet the Lord in the air, or would you be down here scratching your head wondering what's going on?

How much better to go with the Church than to be left behind to face the Tribulation and all the horror that will come upon the earth. Why make it tough for yourself when the Lord wants to make it easy on you? Why not just open your heart and life to Jesus Christ now? Why not just receive Him as your Lord and Saviour and, as He said, be ready? What do you need to be ready? Jesus Christ dwelling in your heart and in your life. For if you will confess with your mouth that Jesus Christ is Lord, and believe in your heart that God has raised Him from the dead, you shall be saved.